NUNAVUT

HARRY BECKETT

Weigl

CALGARY

www.weigl.com

Published by Weigl Educational Publishers Limited
6325 – 10 Street SE
Calgary, Alberta
Canada T2H 2Z9
Web site: http://www.weigl.com

Canadian Cataloguing in Publication Data
Beckett, Harry, 1936-
 Nunavut

 (Eye on Canada)
 Includes Index
 ISBN 1-896990-81-9

 1. Nunavut--Juvenile literature. I. Title. II. Series:
FC4311.2.B43 2000   j971.9'5   C00-911111-5
F1142.4.B43 2000

Printed and bound in the United States
 2 3 4 5 6 7 8 9 0   05 04 03 02

We acknowledge the
financial support of
the Government of
Canada through the
Book Publishing
Industry Development
Program (BPIDP) for
our publishing activities.

Photograph Credits

Every reasonable effort has been made to trace ownership and to obtain
permission to reprint copyright material. The publishers would be pleased to
have any errors or omissions brought to their attention so that they may be
corrected in subsequent printings.

Corel Corporation: pages 3M-R, 7T-L, 11B-L, 11B-R, 11T-L, 14B-L, 20T-R, 26B-L,
26T-R, 27M-L; Lyn Hancock: pages 3B-R, 4B-L, 4B-R, 5M-L, 5T-L, 6B-L, 6M-R,
6T-R, 7B-L, 7T-R, 8T-R, 8B-L, 9T-L, 9B-L, 9B-R, 10M-L, 10B, 12M, 12B, 12T-R,
13T-R, 13B-L, 14B-R, 15B, 15M-L, 16B, 16T-R, 18B, 18T-R, 19T-L, 20B, 20M, 21T-L,
21B, 21B-L, 22B-L, 22M, 23B-L, 23T-L, 23B-R, 24B-L, 24B-R, 25B-L, 25B-R, 27B-L,
27B-R, cover; Hudson's Bay Company Archives, Provincial Archives of Manitoba:
pages 19B-R(N14866), 19B-L(N62-145); Legislative Assembly of Nunavut, Public
Affairs, page 2; National Archives of Canada: pages 3T-R(C11413), 17T-L(C11413),
17B(C2061), 19B-L(PA100771); Nunatsiaq News: page 15T-L.

Project Coordinator
Jill Foran
Design
Lucinda Cage
Warren Clark
Copy Editors
Rennay Craats
Heather Kissock
Layout
Lucinda Cage
Cover Design
Terry Paulhus
Photo Researcher
Joe Nelson

CONTENTS

INTRODUCTION

Before April 1999, Nunavut was a part of the Northwest Territories. Since then, this huge land mass has separated from the Northwest Territories to become a territory of its own. It is by far the largest of any province or territory in Canada, making up about one-fifth of the country's area. Nunavut straddles four time zones as it spreads over the Arctic mainland and islands.

Baffin and Ellesmere islands are now a part of Nunavut, as are the Keewatin, Baffin, and Kitikmeot areas of the Northwest Territories. To the west, the Inuvik and Fort Smith regions establish borders with Nunavut. Manitoba, Hudson Bay, and Quebec border it to the south, and Baffin Bay and the Labrador Sea border it to the east.

Baffin Island is home to Nunavut's capital and many other communities. The island's landscape is made up of tundra, rivers, and glaciers.

EXPLORE CANADA'S ARCTIC
10052N
NUNAVUT
MAR   00

In winter, the lakes and the ground are so frozen that they can be used as temporary roads.

The gold and blue in Nunavut's flag symbolize the riches of land, sea, and sky. The red in the flag is an indication of the territory's ties with Canada.

Getting to Nunavut, and getting around in Nunavut, can be challenging. Because of the territory's rugged terrain, its huge area, and the limited number of people who travel in the north, there are no railways in Nunavut. Outside the towns, there are only about 21 km of road on Baffin Island. Luckily, Nunavut is well served by airlines.

Airlines provide flights from Montreal, Ottawa, Edmonton, and Winnipeg to Iqaluit, Cambridge Bay, or Rankin Inlet. Resolute offers direct flights to Edmonton. Within Nunavut, most communities are linked by scheduled or charter air services.

Boat travel is another method of transportation, but it is limited by the ice that covers much of the water. However, freezing weather can be helpful to other modes of transportation. People can use snowmobiles to get around when the land is snow-covered and the waterways are frozen.

Visitors from Europe fly to Greenland where they connect for a flight to Iqaluit.

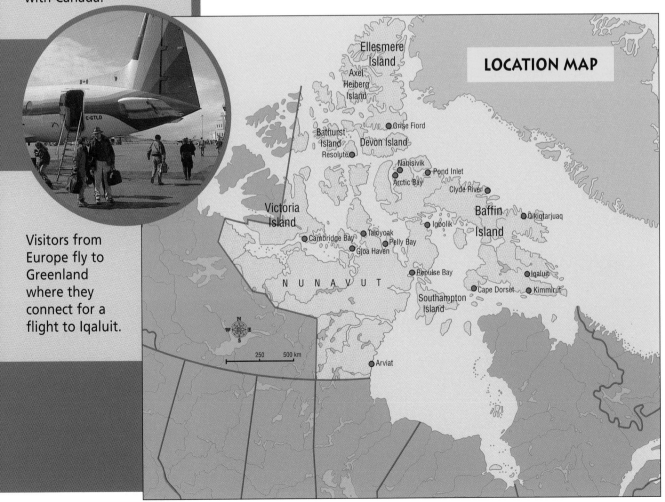

LOCATION MAP

Ellesmere Island
Axel Heiberg Island
Grise Fiord
Bathurst Island
Devon Island
Resolute
Nanisivik
Pond Inlet
Arctic Bay
Clyde River
Victoria Island
Baffin Island
Qikiqtarjuaq
Igoolik
Cambridge Bay
Taloyoak
Pelly Bay
Gjoa Haven
Repulse Bay
Iqaluit
NUNAVUT
Cape Dorset
Kimmirut
Southampton Island
250   500 km
Arviat

Most of Nunavut's many rivers are on the mainland. The Back and the Coppermine rivers flow northward into the Arctic Ocean. The Thelon, Kazan and Dubawnt rivers all eventually flow into Hudson Bay. Because the land is low-lying and irregular, the rivers often widen out to form lakes. The biggest lake on the mainland is Dubawnt Lake.

Most of the rivers on Baffin Island are on the west side. These rivers are short because the sea is never very far away. Nunavut's two largest lakes, Nettilling and Amadjuak, are on Baffin Island. Ellesmere Island also boasts large lakes. Lake Hazen is 72 km long and nearly 10 km wide. It is the largest lake in the area.

Glaciers up to 5 km thick moved across Nunavut during the last Ice Age. As they moved, they scraped the rock bare and then retreated. In some places, they left behind ridges of gravel, called **eskers**. Ice caps 2 km thick still cover much of Ellesmere Island and parts of Devon and Baffin islands.

Wilberforce Falls, on the Hood River near Bathurst Inlet, is the highest waterfall north of the Arctic Circle.

QUICK FACTS

Ice caps and glaciers cover about 150,000 square km of Nunavut.

The introduction of Nunavut marked the first time Canada's map had changed since Newfoundland joined Confederation in 1949.

Many of Nunavut's lakes do not even have names.

The territory's motto is "Nunavut Saginvut," which means "Nunavut our strength."

Inukshuks are human-like stone figures that are believed to have guided travellers and hunters.

At Arctic Bay, which is north of the Arctic Circle, the sun rises on May 4 and does not set again until August 8. In the winter, the sun sets on November 11 and it is not seen again until January 30.

Inuktitut is the official language of the Inuit.

The word "Nunavut" is Inuktitut for "our land." Iqaluit means "place of fish."

The purple saxifrage is the official flower of Nunavut.

The ptarmigan is Nunavut's official bird.

The Mackenzie Delta Dancers perform at a gala celebrating the creation of Nunavut.

Nunavut's vast land region and extensive wilderness is inhabited mostly by Inuit. The struggle to establish an Inuit territory began between the Inuit and the federal government in 1976. It took until 1992 before both sides could agree on all issues, including the western border. In 1993, the land claim agreement was signed, setting the creation of a new territory in motion. Nunavut became an official territory on April 1, 1999.

The land claim that went with this agreement was the largest in Canadian history. It gave the Inuit control over 351,000 square km of Nunavut. It also gave the Inuit mining rights in certain areas, hunting and fishing rights, and payment of about $1.15 billion to the Nunavut Trust over a period of fourteen years. The trust is in charge of protecting and building on this money to ensure a strong Nunavut for years to come.

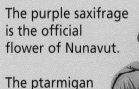

The Nunavut Final Agreement allows Inuit to continue practicing traditi~ hunting met'

LAND AND CLIMATE

Nunavut's landscape is a mixture of mountains, **fjords**, lakes, and **tundra**. The mainland and Baffin Island are part of the **Canadian Shield**. Some of the rocks in this area are more than a billion years old. Further north, the shield is covered with layers of younger rock. Much of the territory's land was shaped by glaciers. The ice sheets reached the Arctic Ocean coastline, creating deep valleys and fjords.

On Axel Heiberg Island, Baffin Island, and the eastern part of Ellesmere Island, mountains range from 1,500 to 2,000 m. The rest of Nunavut is a high, flat plateau gashed by ravines and covered in lakes, **muskeg**, and swamps. The islands to the west are low.

Nunavut's ground is frozen for most of the year, which is an indication of how cold the territory can get. Winters in Nunavut are very long and cold. Daily January temperatures average −20 °Celsius on south Baffin Island and about −37 °C on north Ellesmere Island. Nunavut's short summers can average 21 °C, and for a short time, flowers can bloom. However, cold prevails, and it is possible to build igloos by November.

Nunavut's highest mountain is Mount Barbeau on northern Ellesmere Island. It stands 2,616 m high.

Nunavut's ground is permanently frozen, sometimes to a depth of 500 m. A thin layer of the surface, called the active layer, thaws in summer but re-freezes in winter.

Precipitation in Nunavut ranges from 600 mm in the south to less than 100 mm in the north.

Some areas in Nunavut get less precipitation than the Sahara Desert.

The coldest temperature ever recorded in Nunavut was −57.8 °C at Shepherd Bay in 1973. The warmest temperature was 33.9 °C in Arviat, also in 1973.

The characteristic landscape of Nunavut can be seen along the Duval River as it meets the Pangnirtung Fjord.

NATURAL RESOURCES

The Canadian Shield contains many minerals, but finding and exploiting them in such a remote place as Nunavut is difficult. The expense of transportation and the freezing weather are big challenges to the mining industry. The lead and zinc mines of Nanisivik and Polaris are almost always icebound. Only in summer can ships bring in supplies and carry the ore out.

Mining activities began in the barren lands along the Thelon River after diamonds were discovered there. Plans for more large-scale developments are under way. Nunavut also has large oil and gas deposits in the northern Arctic Ocean. These reserves can only be developed when world oil prices make it possible. Otherwise, the expense of drilling in this area is much too great.

There are no forests or farms in Nunavut.

The most important fish in northern waters is the arctic char.

The Lupin and Polaris mines are called fly-in, fly-out operations. There is no community nearby for workers to live in.

The Lupin gold mine on Contwoyto Lake can only send its products out from January to April on special winter roads.

To make life more enjoyable for the miners, facilities at Polaris Mine include a coffee shop, a swimming pool, and a golf club.

PLANTS AND ANIMALS

Nunavut's infertile, shallow soil is frozen all winter, making life hard for plants. The few plants that live in the territory survive the bitter winters and summers by crowding together. They find shelter in rock crevices or by lying flat to the ground. Lichens and mosses, with some spindly bushes, cover the tundra.

About 200 species of flowers, including dandelions and buttercups, survive to bloom in the long hours of summer sunlight. People and animals take advantage of the blossoming plants. For example, the Inuit eat blueberries, cranberries, and crowberries, while the caribou feast on reindeer lichen.

This young girl enjoys a warm day in Nunavut by collecting flowers.

Despite the cold climate, the tundra comes alive with colourful flowers in the summer.

The Thelon Wildlife Sanctuary is one of the largest and most remote wildlife refuges in North America.

Muskox are found both on the mainland and on most Arctic islands. At one point, the muskox were endangered, but now there are about 47,000 roaming the Nunavut area.

There are different kinds of caribou in Nunavut. The woodland caribou migrate south to the forests, barren ground caribou stay on the tundra, and Peary caribou live on the northern islands.

Nunavut is home to about half the world's polar bears. They feed on the ringed seals that live in the area. Caribou are also abundant, with more than 750,000 living in the territory. The arctic waters are home to beluga whales, **narwhals**, and **bowheads**. Seals and walruses are common Nunavut residents. Hares, squirrels, foxes, weasels, and wolves also make their homes in the area.

Only a few birds survive in the cold tundra. Snowy owls, eider ducks, and gyrfalcons brave the elements and are permanent residents in the territory. Many seabirds will also come north in the spring and summer to breed on the rocky coasts. There is a delicate balance in these barren lands, and each plant and animal plays an important role in the food chain to keep the ecosystem strong.

Polar bears in the Nunavut area spend most of the year roaming the sea ice.

The rough-legged hawk is one type of bird found in Nunavut. It nests on cliff sides and hunts in the open tundra.

TOURISM

Many people travel to Nunavut to take in its unique scenery. Wilderness canoe trips down the Thelon River allow visitors close-up views of muskox, caribou, white arctic wolves, golden eagles, rough-legged hawks, and owls. Tourists can marvel at the spectacular wilderness, mountain fortresses, and fascinating wildlife of Auyuittuq National Park Reserve and Ellesmere Island National Park Reserve.

In summer, visitors can venture to the floe edge, where the ice meets the open sea. Here they can see the shrimp that come to eat plankton, and the seals and whales that feed on the shrimp. There may even be polar bears lurking close by.

Visitors centres in various communities have demonstrations of everyday activities that took place in traditional Inuit summer camps. Others interpret the traditions of a thousand years of Inuit life in Nunavut.

National parks such as Auyuittuq are popular destinations for tourists.

The spring ice floes are not only a tourist attraction. Polar bears, seals, and walruses also use them as a hunting base or to relax in the sun.

QUICK FACTS

Bathurst Inlet's interpretive centre for beginner and expert birders is considered a world-class facility.

The remains of stone fox traps and thousand- year-old dwellings line the coast, attracting history buffs.

Nunavut has tourist camps where visitors can learn traditional craft-making.

The Nunatta Sunakkutaangit Museum in Iqaluit has displays that explain the history of south Baffin Island. It also exhibits a variety of Inuit art and clothing.

INDUSTRY

Inuit art ranges from paintings and carvings to jewellery and dolls. In many cases, the art is a reflection of Inuit culture.

The three operational mines in Nunavut provide about 965 jobs. However, the territory has not yet had time to train many engineers and specialists, so most of the employees are non-residents of Nunavut. Only about 15 percent of the employees at the mines are Inuit.

Once the new government of Nunavut took power, office buildings and houses were needed to accommodate the people employed. The construction industry continues to grow because of the business that self-government has generated. Houses are also needed because Inuit continue to move to where the jobs are being created.

The sale of Inuit art is an important industry in Nunavut. A large part of the territory's economy is based on exporting this art to other places around the world. Until the 1940s, Inuit art was almost completely unavailable to those outside the Arctic. Through marketing projects, the popularity and demand for Inuit art spread all over the world. Today, a large number of Inuit artists earn their livings by selling their work.

GOODS AND SERVICES

Almost no goods are produced for sale in Nunavut. Many items have to be imported from the south, which makes them very expensive. For example, imported foods cost about one-third more than they do in southern Canada due to the added shipping costs. In more remote communities, such as Grise Fiord, costs are even higher. For this reason, locally caught fish and game are very important. Food that is caught locally and eaten traditionally is called country food. It makes up more than half of what is eaten in Nunavut.

The governments of Canada and Nunavut are the biggest employers in the territory. The treaty that made Nunavut a territory states that 85 percent of government workers are to be Inuit. The treaty also says that Inuit companies must have increased participation in government contracts. The government hires private companies to build office complexes. Other companies provide services including retail stores and taxis to accommodate the needs of government employees and other residents.

Despite the cost of imported items, stores still carry candy, books, and even videos.

Iqaluit's Parnaivik Building is a mini-mall that houses government offices, a coffee shop, and a fabric store.

Healthcare services in Nunavut are provided by the government. There is one hospital in Iqaluit and about fourteen community health centres throughout Nunavut's regions. These centres offer nursing, children's welfare, and counselling services.

Five percent of government employees work in education, which is also managed directly in the regions. All communities have schools, and the main community colleges in Nunavut are the Nanatta Campus of Nunavik Arctic College in Iqaluit and the Nunavut Research Institute. The institute provides guidance in traditional knowledge, science, research, and technology.

To maintain the Inuit culture, the government is building an Inuktituk curriculum and training Inuit teachers. Good classes in Inuktituk are necessary because it is the working language of the government.

The Igloolik Research Institute is part of the Nunavik Arctic College. It is also a good example of Nunavut's interesting architecture.

Nunavut gets its news from the CBC Northern Service and the *Nunatsiaq News* newspaper.

The service industry is important in Nunavut. People working in the service sector do things for other people. Waiters, doctors, government officials, sales clerks, and lawyers are all service employees.

FIRST NATIONS

The pre-Dorset people arrived in the Canadian Arctic about 4,500 years ago. These people formed small groups to follow the caribou and seal, and they used tools and weapons made of flint and bone. They lived in tents made of animal skin.

The Dorset people emerged about 2,500 years ago. In the spring, they hunted walruses, caribou, small mammals, and seals. They caught fish in the summer, and trapped seals in the fall and winter. Some of the food they caught was stored in **caches** for the long winter seasons.

Nunavut's present-day Inuit are descended from the Thule, who originally migrated from Alaska. The summer homes of the Thule were tents made of animal skins, but their winter homes were solid structures. The Thule hunted for game with bows and arrows or spears. In summer, they hunted for whales from kayaks and fished with **tridents** and hooks.

The Thule's graves consisted of piles of stones, with the remains of the person and their belongings placed nearby.

Thule winter homes were sunk into the ground. They had a stone floor, a whale bone or stone frame, and a roof of seal skin. Houses were covered with sod and heated by seal or whale oil burned in a stone lamp.

The Thule may have been the first peoples to use dog sleds.

Frobisher took what he thought was gold back to England. It proved to be iron pyrites or "fool's gold."

The strait between Greenland and Baffin Island is named for John Davis.

The crews of Davis' four ships played a soccer game on the ice with the Inuit.

Many explorers died because they did not learn how to survive in Nunavut's harsh climate.

Between the years of 1903 and 1906, Roald Amundson became the first person to successfully navigate a ship through the Northwest Passage.

EXPLORERS

The first European to reach Nunavut was an English explorer named Sir Martin Frobisher. He sailed west from the Atlantic Ocean in search of the **Northwest Passage**. In 1576, he landed on Baffin Island and named the area Frobisher Strait. He returned to the area two more times in search of gold.

The search for the Northwest Passage brought many other explorers to the area. In the 1580s, John Davis tried his luck at finding the passage, but ice floes blocked his route. In 1610, Henry Hudson believed he had succeeded in finding the Northwest Passage when he entered the bay now named for him. His ship became iced in, and the cold climate led to an angry crew. His crew **mutinied** and Hudson and several others were set adrift in a small boat. They were never seen again.

In 1845, Captain John Franklin was also determined to find the Northwest Passage. He set out with 129 British navy

sailors. His ships became stuck in ice and the crews were lost when they left the ships. The British Navy mapped most of the Arctic islands and straits while searching for Franklin and his crew.

Henry Hudson had gone on many earlier expeditions in search of the Northwest Passage before his disappearance in 1610.

EARLY SETTLERS

Basque and Portuguese fishers came to Nunavut in the 1500s for the fish and whales, but they did not settle there. Whalers continued to come for four centuries in search of whale oil and baleen. Whale oil was used in the lamps of Europe and North America, and baleen, the bony plates from the whale, did many of the jobs that plastic does today.

By the 1850s, whalers had established whaling stations and spent the winter in the Arctic so they could be there when the season began. This changed some traditional Inuit ways. Many Inuit began to stay and work with the whalers instead of going inland in the summer to hunt. The Inuit did most of the whaling and traded oil for European goods. Guns, metal pots, cloth, utensils, and alcohol became important to many Inuit communities. But contact with Europeans had a price. Many Inuit died from diseases brought by Europeans.

European whaling crews were eager to recruit the Inuit because of their excellent hunting skills.

Education by the missionaries went on until the 1960s when the government began to build schools.

According to traditional Inuit belief, shamans are men or women who bring health and prosperity and know the secrets of magic and religion.

The Inuit called Reverend Peck "Uqammak," which means "the one who speaks well." The script he developed is still used today.

Missionaries followed the whalers and traders to the eastern Arctic. It was their aim to convert the Inuit from their belief in **shamans** to Christianity.

Reverend Edmund Peck set up the first mission in 1894 on Black Lead Island near Pangnirtung in the Cumberland Sound. He helped develop a written form of Inuktitut using symbols. He then translated the Bible into this Inuit language.

Other missionaries travelled to Inuit camps spreading the word of Christianity and discouraging the use of shamans. The Inuit adopted many aspects of Christianity, and sometimes they formed their own religions by mixing various religious ideas. At the same time, they lost many of their traditional beliefs.

The churches also set up the first schools and hospitals. During the 1920s and 1930s, five residential schools were established. Children as young as five were taken away from their own culture to learn the Christian way of life.

Reverend Edmund Peck helped develop a written form of Inuktituk. He also set up the first permanent mission in the area.

POPULATION

Before 1999, the Northwest Territories had two main regions. The west was the partly forested Mackenzie Valley, populated by Dene, Métis, Inuit, and non-aboriginal people. The east was mainly barren, and 85 percent of its inhabitants were Inuit.

In 1999, the east became Nunavut, and was divided into three regions. Eastern and northern Nunavut are called Qikiqtaaluk, or the Baffin region. Southern Nunavut and the area near Hudson Bay are called Kivalliq, or Keewatin. Central and western Nunavut are called Kitikmeot.

The Baffin region, which includes almost all the islands, is the largest and the most heavily populated region. There are twenty-five communities in Nunavut. Eight of them are on Baffin Island.

The majority of Canada's Inuit live in Nunavut.

QUICK FACTS

Iqaluit has about 4,700 residents.

Until 1987, Iqaluit was known as Frobisher Bay.

Canada's most northerly community is Grise Fiord, on Ellesmere Island.

The Inuit make up 85 percent of Nunavut's population. The rest of the population is made up mostly of people of British and European descent.

The government building in Iqaluit has wooden arches formed to represent an igloo. It also has sealskin-covered benches instead of desks in the meeting chamber.

Elders, with their skills and traditional knowledge, play an important role in all areas of Inuit life and politics.

Paul Ikalik became the first premier of Nunavut in 1999.

POLITICS AND GOVERNMENT

A territory is different from a province. A province owns its own land and has powers that are set out in Confederation. A territory, on the other hand, is created through federal law, and the federal government owns the land. Also, the federal government can make decisions in a territory on matters such as education, whereas provinces can make their own decisions and policies. A territory cannot vote on changes to the Canadian Constitution.

The Nunavut territorial government has an elected Legislative Assembly with nineteen members and a cabinet of ministers overseeing the activities of ten departments. Some departments, like the Department of Culture, Language, Elders, and Youth, are concerned with maintaining Inuit traditions. The departments and agencies are spread around the communities of Nunavut so that they will all receive a share of the $1.15 billion granted to the new territory by the federal government. This will also allow regions to make decisions according to their local needs.

The government of Nunavut is based in Iqaluit.

CULTURAL GROUPS

The Inuit culture stems from an ancient **nomadic** society where survival depended both on teamwork and on respect for one's natural surroundings. Working together was vital to surviving in the harsh climate of the North. Today, the Inuit in Nunavut continue to respect their environment and to believe in the importance of sharing. The sharing of **game** and fish among families is still a vital part of Inuit culture. Many Inuit believe that food tastes better when it is shared with family and friends.

Food in Nunavut is very different from most Canadian dishes. Among the most popular foods are arctic char, caribou, and muskox, which tastes like beef. Raw seal is a traditional dish. During a meal, men and women get different parts of the seal. Other favourites include maktaaq, which consists of the outer skin of the whale served raw, and dips such as aalu, which is made up of caribou or seal meat, fat, blood, and ptarmigan intestines. Misiraq, which is aged seal blubber, and nirukkaq, which are the contents of a caribou's stomach, are other unique dips.

Many families gather to enjoy raw seal during a communal feast celebrating the Christmas season.

An expert seal hunter lunges his spear at a seal just beneath the water's surface.

QUICK FACTS

Inuit peoples live across the northern Arctic, from Alaska to Greenland, in eight main groups. They speak up to twenty different dialects of Inuktituk and can usually understand each other.

About 71 percent of Nunavut's population speak Inuktitut.

English is spoken by 24 percent of Nunavut's population, and French is spoken by about 2 percent.

The word "Inuit" means "people" in Inuktitut. "Inuk" means "one person."

The Inuit burn whale or seal oil on a stone lamp, or qulliq, to heat and light igloos. As a symbol, it represents the light and warmth of the family and community.

The Inuit show their love for children very openly, allowing relatives to adopt one of their children if they have many. Traditionally, elders name the babies after relatives or people they admire.

Inuit names were too hard for missionaries to pronounce, so they gave them biblical names. The government simply gave them numbers stamped on a disc and looped around their necks.

Some Inuit still follow the traditional nomadic life, while many others have moved into the world of business, helping to develop Nunavut through politics, teaching, medicine, and broadcasting.

The language of the Inuit is Inuktitut. It is spoken throughout Nunavut, but **dialects** and accents vary from region to region. In Kitikmeot, or western Nunavut, the name of the Inuit language is Inuinnaqtun.

A large portion of the Inuit population in Nunavut speaks English, but all over the territory, Inuit strive to keep their traditional language alive. They have also added new words to their vocabulary, some of which are related to the English word. For example, when European explorers arrived, the Inuit were introduced to items like sugar and paper. They adopted these words into their own language, and now "sukaq" and "paipaaq" are Inuktitut words.

Snowmobiles, rifles, schools, and permanent housing have had a great influence on the Inuit way of life. Although older Inuit speak only Inuktituk, most younger adults are comfortable in both the Inuit and mainstream Canadian worlds. More and more, young people are taking advantage of modern technology, including the Internet.

People in Nunavut have been able to balance tradition with European culture. For example, children's school years are based around the hunting seasons.

ARTS AND ENTERTAINMENT

Art is a valued part of Inuit life. It ranges from sculpture and fabric-making to art prints and jewellery. The Inuit carve in soapstone, **serpentine**, marble, ivory, and bone. Early sculptures usually represented local activities, mythical figures, or the shapes and spirits of animals. Printmaking, which is a growing Inuit art form, also tells stories of wilderness survival, traditional myths, and shamans.

Another traditional art form among the Inuit is storytelling. Much of Inuit history is preserved through this favourite pastime. At celebrations, people tell stories with important themes and messages or that detail the hardships of hunting. Celebrations also involve singing, drumming, and plenty of food.

With the introduction of modern tools, carving became an easier and more profitable industry for Inuit artists.

Music has always been an important part of Inuit life. For centuries, drum dancing has welcomed visitors and celebrated births, weddings, deaths, and successful hunts. Singers, usually women, would sit in a circle while drummers played. Men would volunteer to dance in the circle. Drum dancing is now performed mainly for tourists and on ceremonial occasions.

Another fascinating form of Inuit music is throat singing. This incredible art form involves two or three singers, usually women. These women stand face to face and make rhythmic noises by breathing out from the throat. The sound that resonates between the singers often represents the sounds of birds or animals.

Some of Nunavut's musicians have earned acclaim beyond the territory. Arviat's Susan Aglukark has won fame all over Canada by mixing Inuit chants with pop music in English and Inuktituk. Her songs discuss the discrimination against Inuit peoples and her own personal tragedies and successes. They also touch on Inuit rituals and values and the hardships of northern life. Aglukark has won an Aboriginal Achievement Award and a Juno Award for best new solo artist. The throat singing duo, Tudjaat, has appeared in concert and on record with Susan Aglukark.

Susan Aglukark is a famous singer. Her music incorporates many aspects of traditional Inuit music such as rhythmic drumming.

Inuit music has been brought to wide audiences through media coverage and events such as The Great Northern Arts Festival and the Inummarit Music Festival.

European whalers and traders brought the country fiddle, accordion, and mouth organ to Nunavut. Country and western and gospel music are also very popular.

Square dancing is a popular pastime all over Nunavut.

Pioneer Inuit musicians like Charlie Panigoniak have a wide following of fans.

SPORTS

Activities such as camping, kayaking, dogsledding, snowmobiling, hunting, and fishing are considered recreational sports in southern Canada. In Nunavut, they are more than that. These sports are a part of the traditional Inuit way of life. The people of Nunavut also love sports such as hockey, curling, and badminton. They even enjoy a round of golf now and then!

Traditional Inuit games are both a diversion to Nunavut's long, cold months and a way to stay fit. Many of the games are based on skills that were once needed to survive in the Arctic. One of the most popular games is the high kicks. Among the types of high kicks are the two-foot and one-foot high kicks, and the Alaskan high kick. The one and two-foot high kicks involve jumping up, kicking an object that is suspended in the air, and landing in a certain way. The Alaskan high kick requires great skill and wrist strength, as part of the kick involves balancing the entire body on one wrist.

Dogsledding has been a part of life in Nunavut since the arrival of the Thule people from Alaska.

QUICK FACTS

Cross-country skiing is a popular pastime among Nunavut's residents and visitors. Skiers can witness Nunavut's wildlife up close as they glide along.

The kayak is a closed-deck hunting canoe, usually designed for one person. It is made of driftwood with willow ribs and covered in de-haired sealskin or caribou skin.

Each community has a Hamlet Day to celebrate spring. It is almost always a combination of traditional and modern games and races. Some even have "blindfolded human dog team" races.

Toonik Tyme is Nunavut's largest festival of traditional Inuit games. The games take place in Iqaluit every spring. Igloo building, snowmobile and dog-team races, entertainment, and feasting are all a part of the fun.

Other important athletic competitions are held throughout the territory. The Midnight Sun Marathon celebrates the longest day of the year and attracts runners from all over the world. One hundred runners from Canada, the United States, Europe, and Australia are invited to run in the 10-km, 32-km, 42-km, or 84-km races between Arctic Bay and Nanisivik. The Midnight Sun Golf Tournament at Pelly Bay is played on a home-made course. Golfers tee off on rugs loaned by local families.

The Kitikmeot Northern Games in summer have unique Good Man and Good Woman contests in family skills, such as tea boiling, duck plucking, seal skinning, and bannock making.

Every two years, Nunavut's athletes join with athletes from other Arctic regions for the Arctic Winter Games.

The snow snake is an event in which an athlete throws a spear as far as possible down a snow channel.

Each society brings a small group of cultural artists to the Arctic Games. A display of visual arts and crafts and a cultural program run for the length of the games.

The Kitikmeot Northern Games include many traditional Inuit games such as the pole twist and various jump kicks.

EYE ON CANADA

Nunavut is one of the ten provinces and three territories that make up Canada. Compare Nunavut's statistics with those of other provinces and territories. What differences and similarities can you find?

Northwest Territories

Entered Confederation:
July 15, 1870

Capital: Yellowknife

Area: 171,918 sq km

Population: 41,606
Rural: 58 percent
Urban: 42 percent

Population Density:
0.24 people per sq km

Yukon

Entered Confederation:
June 13, 1898

Capital: Whitehorse

Area: 483,450 sq km

Population: 30,633
Rural: 40 percent
Urban: 60 percent

Population Density:
0.06 people
per sq km

British Columbia

Entered Confederation:
July 20, 1871

Capital: Victoria

Area: 947,800 sq km

Population: 4,023,100
Rural: 18 percent
Urban: 82 percent

Population Density:
4.24 people
per sq km

Alberta

Entered Confederation:
September 1, 1905

Capital: Edmonton

Area: 661,190 sq km

Population: 2,964,689
Rural: 20 percent
Urban: 80 percent

Population Density:
4.48 people
per sq km

Saskatchewan

Entered Confederation:
September 1, 1905

Capital: Regina

Area: 652,330 sq km

Population: 1,027,780
Rural: 28 percent
Urban: 72 percent

Population Density:
1.57 people per sq km

Manitoba

Entered Confederation
July 15, 1870

Capital: Winnipeg

Area: 649,950 sq km

Population: 1,143,509
Rural: 28 percent
Urban: 72 percent

Population Density:
1.76 people per sq km

Nunavut

Entered Confederation:
April 1, 1999

Capital: Iqaluit

Area: 1,900,000 sq km

Population: 27,039

Population Density:
0.014 people per sq km

CANADA

Confederation:
July 1,1867

Capital: Ottawa

Area: 9,203,054 sq km

Population: 30,491,294
Rural: 22 percent
Urban: 78 percent

Population Density:
3.06 people
per sq km

Quebec

Entered Confederation:
July 1, 1867

Capital: Quebec City

Area: 1,540,680 sq km

Population: 7,345,390
Rural: 21 percent
Urban: 79 percent

Population Density:
4.77 people per sq km

Newfoundland & Labrador

Entered Confederation:
March 31, 1949

Capital: St. John's

Area: 405,720 sq km

Population: 541,000
Rural: 43 percent
Urban: 57 percent

Population Density:
1.33 people
per sq km

Prince Edward Island

Entered Confederation:
July 1, 1873

Capital:
Charlottetown

Area: 5,660 sq km

Population: 137,980
Rural: 56 percent
Urban: 44 percent

Population Density:
24.38 people
per sq km

Ontario

Entered Confederation:
July 1, 1867

Capital: Toronto

Area: 1,068,580 sq km

Population: 11,513,808
Rural: 17 percent
Urban: 83 percent

Population Density:
10.77 people per sq km

New Brunswick

Entered Confederation:
July 1, 1867

Capital: Fredericton

Area: 73,440 sq km

Population: 754,969
Rural: 51 percent
Urban: 49 percent

Population Density:
10.28 people per sq km

Nova Scotia

Entered Confederation:
July 1, 1867

Capital: Halifax

Area: 55,490 sq km

Population: 939,791
Rural: 45 percent
Urban: 55 percent

Population Density:
16.94 people
per sq km

BRAIN TEASERS

Test your knowledge of Nunavut
by trying to answer these
mind-boggling brain teasers!

1 True or False: Polar bears in Nunavut will often feast on penguins in the area.

2 True or False: Nunavut has more airplane boardings per person than any other province or territory in the country.

3 Make a Guess: What Nunavut sea creature is also known as the unicorn of the sea?

4 True or False: In Nunavut, there are only eighty vehicles per 1000 people.

5 True or False: There are no tanning salons in Nunavut.

6 Make a Guess: What does the Inuktitut phrase "Qanuippit" mean in English?

7 Make a Guess: Why is it so hard to pave roads in Nunavut?

8 Make a Guess: Are there mosquitoes in Nunavut?

1. False. Penguins do not live in the Arctic. They live in Antarctica, in the southern part of the world.

2. True. There are more than five times as many airline boardings in Nunavut than in the rest of the country.

3. The narwhal. This creature has an ivory tusk that twists from its upper jaw.

4. True. Snowmobiles also outnumber cars in Nunavut.

5. False. Iqaluit has two tanning salons.

6. How are you?

7. The ground in Nunavut is always frozen, which makes paving very difficult and expensive.

8. Yes. Parts of Nunavut are infested with mosquitoes and other insects during the short summer months.

GLOSSARY

bowhead: a type of whale with a very large head and a lower lip that curves up in a bow on each side

caches: places for storing supplies

Canadian Shield: a region of ancient rock that encircles Hudson Bay and covers a large portion of Canada's mainland

dialect: a form of speech characteristic to a certain region

eskers: curving ridges of sand or gravel probably deposited by meltwaters

fjords: long, deep, and narrow sea inlets formed by glaciers

game: animals, fish, and birds that are hunted for sport

muskeg: an area of swamp or marsh

mutinied: to have rebelled against an authority

narwhals: whales that swim in the arctic seas. The male narwhal has a huge tusk that extends from a tooth in the upper jaw.

nomadic: a way of life that involves moving from place to place in search of food and water

Northwest Passage: a short-cut route for ships from the Atlantic to the Pacific Ocean

serpentine: a green or spotted mineral resembling a serpent's skin

shamans: medicine men or priests believed to have spiritual powers

trident: a spear that has three prongs

tundra: an Arctic or subarctic plain with a permanently frozen subsoil

BOOKS

Hancock, Lyn. *Hello Canada: Nunavut*. Minneapolis: Lerner Publishing Group, 1995.

Keen, Jared. *Iqaluit*. From the *Canadian Cities* series. Calgary: Weigl Educational Publishers, 2000.

Soublière, Marion. *The 1999 Nunavut Handbook*. Nunavut: Nortext, 1998.

WEB SITES

Official Nunavut Site
http://www.nunavut.com

The Nunavut Handbook
http://www.arctic-travel.com

Government of Nunavut
http://www.gov.nu.ca

Some Web sites stay current longer than others. To find more Nunavut Web sites, use your Internet search engine to look up such topics as "Nunavut," "Iqaluit," "the Arctic," "Inuit," or any other topic you want to research.

INDEX